CW00869622

A Path to Cornwall

Rick Howarth

Copyright © 2015 Rick Howarth

Cover Design, Original Screen Print
"Contemplation" by Rick Howarth

All rights reserved.

ISBN: 1503300382
ISBN-13: 978-1503300385

Rick Howarth

Dedicated to the late Sam Blewett of Porthleven,
a teaching colleague, friend & gentleman.

ACKNOWLEDGMENTS

With thanks to my son Christopher, without whose technical knowledge and assistance this publication would not have been possible.

INTRODUCTION

By retirement one would normally expect to have identified, explored and developed any creative potential one had but it was only as recently as August 2014 that I wrote my first verse. Since then I have hardly stopped! I would encourage anyone who feels they might have some creative potential lurking inside of them to explore it, in my case I have found it very rewarding.

I offer you the results of my new found inspiration in this little book. Some of the poems are specifically Cornish others obliquely so, ultimately I have lived and worked in this magical County for most of my life, but some refer to my childhood in Lancashire and other great landscape love Cumbria and the Lake District. I make no apology for stating that my poetry aims to please, you will find an almost total predominance of rhyme simply because rhyme and metered verse is my preferred medium. If I may quote the celebrated American poet Robert Frost, *"Free verse is like playing tennis with the net down".*

I love most to write about nature, about the landscape and the creatures that reside in it, including people.

The poems are roughly grouped by themes, for example the natural world, personal experiences, family, love, Cornwall, etc. I hope you enjoy them it will be a great thrill for me to think you will.

A Remote Cornish Beach in Summer

Who loves those days when the sun is hazed,
And the seas unruffled with its mirrored glaze
Showing every ripple and fish that moves
In the currents stream swept surface ooze.

And the tide on the beach treads soft and slow
Leaving hardly a footprint as it goes
Where the dark sand that each sea fall makes
Is quickly absorbed to its flaxen state.

When the sand is warmly soft and gold
And the seagull's plaintiff call is bold
As no other sound competes for space
In air as soft as a mothers embrace.

And you lay by a bed of scented pinks
As rustling reeds their music links
To a skylarks distant worshipping praise
To sunlit, happy, palliate days.

And the amphitheatre of the cliffs
Reduces all the world to this,
Sea, sand and skies sensuous ideal
Caresses, body and soul to heal.

Cornwall. Sailing. Percuil.

Sloe hedged path of grass and moss,
Granite channelled stream embossed
Upon the creeping mud and slime,
The minion vessels close confined.

Silence thick in colds grey air
We start our great adventure there,
Our oars caress the roading stream,
Onward to a conscious dream.

Infant rivers lapsing stride
Directs our progress o'er the tide
Expanding to a wider reach,
Pinioned ghosts there fetch and breach

Here birds awakened from their sleep
Call and cry for daylights reap
That lies upon that island strand
Of flaxen sea fed nurturing sand.

Ahead the mist is channelled through
Our carriage now comes to view,
Dipping oars more regular beat
Pennanted bearer there to meet.

We climb aboard our hobbled steed
To give her flight and wings for speed,
Quick aloft her wings are set,
Restlessly she veers and frets.

Tether binds wind gifted strength,
Attendant masters tread her length
To coil and cleat and needs attend
So safely on our journey send.

Now from the taut grey chain is freed,
Unrestrained she gathers speed,
Outbound to the open sea,
Adventure wed to liberty.

Heligan Woods

As I walked through Heligan woods
A butterfly passed by when I stood,
Erratic flight through dank cold air
The sun had made false promise there.

Awakened to a starving land,
Bereft of nectars saving hand,
Sun veiled and like the moon disguised,
No warmth and only light provides.

The trees have wept their leaves away
In Autumn breezes greedy play,
The village masked beyond those trees
Now once more shows its face to me.

White cottages clinging to the steep
That guides its river to the deep,
Land gives its flowing gift for free
To harbour walled encircled sea.

A rarer breed therein reside,
Men of the sea and net and tide,
Close knit and guarding of their art,
Defining land and sea apart.

They know the set of every tide,
Where fishes swim and lobsters hide,
But time and circumstance decline
Means few and fewer are inclined.

Tourists seeking a land of bliss
Village and beach with sun to kiss
An easier quarry these men see
Less chance, less danger, constancy

But as I ponder on these things
Music's paradise to me sings
And Kauffman betters my attempts
His beauteous voice by heaven sent.

The haunting beauty of lament
Sum-mates all music's sacrament
I rest my pen from poetic waste
Humbled there to know my place

*The musical reference is to Jonas Kaufmann
singing Lamento di Federico-L'Arlesiana (Bizet)*

A Cornish Day Out in a vintage MG

Sitting on the gravelled drive,
Gleaming chrome with the ivory hide,
Promising us a trip through time
When down the steep banked lanes we glide.

The engines voice even and strong
As happily we roll along,
To the peaceful ferry place,
Cross the rivers smooth embrace.

Go steeply up the winding hill
Past Copelands house, visitor filled,
Onwards towards the climbing road
Which leads to Penryn's entrance door.

But we've more distant place in mind
So progress high 'bove Constantine,
Our next objective Helston town
And by the airfield skirting round.

Roads end here, lanes our route again,
Rurally tracking, bend on bend,
Past Mullion to the Lizard white
Where by the lighthouse we alight.

The high set car-park gives the view
Of sea and land with charm imbued
So picnic basket on the ground
And drinks and food are spread around.

Two little hounds watch bites and sips
They look hangdog and lick their lips
So you abandon your respite
Then each of them can have a bite.

Conscience salved you finish your meal,
By now their thirst must be repealed
Then finally you all are fed
Your actions now are stomach led.

Essential after such a fest
To aid digestion with a rest.
Six mile walk previously foretold?
Recumbent, Morpheus's hand we hold!

The sun is now at ten past three,
Awake then from our reverie,
"The dogs look tired". Deceitful say,
"We'll do the walk another day".

So once again all is prepared
To mount our fleet foot oily bird,
The dogs settle themselves with ease
And we fit in there where they please!

We creep back down the narrow lane
Through the villages tourist bane
Speed home over valley and rise
Refreshed by all that exercise!

Late Summer

Woods and fields are veiled with silk,
The sea and sky are one.
Delicate brushstrokes sweep the blue
To gently mask the sun,
And nature's voice is softly warm,
Caressing and benign,
Winged children play and sing
Their praise to this the time
Before autumn and winter
Reap their harvest from the wild
And strip away the green and gold
To rest their lovely child.
They will stand aside for Spring,
Awake from healing sleep,
Kiss to life again with love
The beauty we all seek.

A Garden Where I Go

There is a garden where I go,
A sheltered bower there to keep
Where crocus and narcissi grow
Deep into winter's sun starved sleep.

Its cropped high hedges face the sea,
A view far distant and blue veiled,
When wintry winds blow hard and free
It shelters all from deathly gale.

Slate interlocked a courtyard makes
And in the centre of this bed
Cast iron fountains water rakes
On fishes clothed in gilt and red.

Tall blasted trees 'round naked stand
Where noisy rooks still hold their place
And rasp their call for kinder land
When sun melts cloud and shows its face.

Shrubs and flowers with footed root
Held firm in red grooved pots of clay
Are pond edge lined like sentries mute
To hold the water's splashing play

And men hold forth, tell of a scene,
Sat on wrought seats for comfort placed,
That in the night to dawns first gleam
By time-took gardeners here is graced.

Pendower Storm

Grey clouds fold and mask the light
Gifts day the solemnity of night
As on the beach the roaring crests
A rhythmic beat makes manifest.

Coppiced slopes do winds song cry
Hymn greyed and sodden like the sky,
Along it on grooved slate brown beach
Channels pools where sand is breached

Spumed white sea in valleys dance
As glass green mountains make advance
To act creations other age
When brother ice did land assuage.

Reworks the soft and yielding sand
To sculpt the step twixt sea and land,
Imposing strength without relent
Thus the seas energies are spent

Green giants there defiant stand
Rooting hold upon the land,
Deep their grasp within their birth
Embraced, embracing of the earth.

Where man has fixed to love the sea
His dwelling's in adversity,
Gale forces giant to his small
Robbed his kingdom lost to fall.

Here vanity is all for nought
When against nature it is wrought,
The conqueror of the world bow knee
Vanquished by the wind and sea.

Sea Adventure

I venture on a falling tide,
My little ship the current rides
Down river to the encircled sea,
From Carrick Roads soon to be free.

Beneath Saint Anthony hoist the sails
And now the boat leans to its rail
As winds hand grips and gives it course
I head away from lands breeze force.

Now swiftly run the green salt road,
Here once the Pilgrim Fathers strode,
Drake set foreign mariners dread
And Packets news the Empire read.

The lift and fall of my wood stead
Increases on westerly breeze,
Sheet in the sails and head her forth
Upon my salt sprayed bucking course.

To the south west I see the teeth
Of that great hungry Manacles beast
That's fed upon the bones of man
Since first he ventured to the van.

Now on my bow motioning slow
Its great steel marker buoy sings low
A mournful lonely elegy.
To all the souls there lost at sea

I think of tragic emigrants
Set off with hope and confidence
In wooden ships with east set sails
Then wind and water set deaths rails

Not long to think upon these things
As now the salt lain wind loud sings
About I circle, homeward tack
My little ship will carry me back

And now the sea is on my stern,
'Tis time for me my bread to earn,
I surf the hissing chasing green
Within whose troughs no distance seen.

A time be sure to keep one's head
As swiftly homeward I am sped,
She must not turn or those high waves
Will swamp me to a watery grave.

Rick Howarth

But all who love to sail the sea
Will sing that such adversity
Is the essence of the great depart
From routines soul diminishing art.

Soon the adventures close to end,
Above me is the mariner's friend,
Atop the cliffs the lighthouse stands
Welcoming home to Cornwall's land.

So now I'm back to furl the sails,
To start the engines grumbling wail,
Percuil my mooring there I keep,
Both boat and I to bed and sleep.

The Carrick Roads

The gentle slopes of velvet green
Around a broad reached estuary scene,
The silent rippling river seeps
Along its banks towards the deep.
And on its sucking, clinging ooze
Rest sleeping ships with absent crews,
Close by their beds with scull and wind
Fly little boats on waters sing.
Outward towards the brine soaked air
They fish their trade with sails set fair,
Each time loved, wood hulled, canvassed craft
For generations at the task.
Here men encrusted with their take
They pull and lift and shellfish rake.
Along affront the Royal Keep
The wider river bellies deep
So giant merchant ships can ply
And to the Docks the whole world tie.
They rest their sides, are fed and feed
At granite berths with planks and weed,
Served by the cranes their goods they spill,
Then take new cargo holds to fill.
To sail a clarion calls dispersed,
Loud enough to waken the earth,
Echoes across the sea around,
Heard across valley, sea and town
The monstrous weight of floating steel
Demands its route without appeal,

The creeping giant silent sets
Across the shallow sandstone steps.
Now freed at last and unrestrained
It points its bow its route to claim.

The Heligan Gardener. A tribute

Today once more on poet's seat
I sat and mused a world deplete,
With trees gale bared of autumns gold
Where winter smokes caress unfolds.

Grey ghosts that rose to touch the sky,
Spirits of men destined to die,
Who could not know the coming trial?
In wars defile their lives made vile.

They worked within a landscape fine,
Grew pineapples and clementine,
They loved the earth and practised skill,
To crop and nurture natures will.

And then beyond enclosing walls
They heard the bugles distant call,
It sang adventure far from home,
A promise of the world to roam.

March with friends to a distant land,
Be part of that heroic band,
For Country, Duty, to be men,
It could not tell of horrors ken.

It did not tell of trench and mud,
Of fear and deaths hand drenched in blood,
Of bomb and bullet, gassed and blind,
Each day expecting end of time.

A war unknown through all before,
Destruction's scale immense in gore,
Where fragile man was torn apart
By shell and steal thrust to the heart.

Epilogue

A fevered soldier shivering cold,
His rain drenched coat around him folds,
His feet diseased by constant wet
In fitful sleep he moans and frets.

He's once more in those gardens green
Of apple orchards, ranks of beans,
The vegetables and vivid flowers,
With friends he works productive hours.

The sun is blessing all the earth,
His wife and children filled with mirth,
Happy in a golden world
In distant Heligan's warmth enfurled.

The mine that took his life away
As in the slime wet trench he lay,
Buried deep within the ground
His earthly guise is never found.

Absolved his spirit now can be
Familiar paths he wanders free,
Again his world to love and roam,
The Heligan gardener's home.

A Copse by the Sea

Whisper me, caressing breeze
And in my ear sings song of seas,
Bow that brushes o'er the branch
Play melodies and me entrance,
Dancing round and through the grass
Transforming fields to shimmering glass
And where the sun would burn the eye
Your cooling hands will mist the sky

On the estuary see its tread
Where other breezes skip and thread
To smooth and texture in their play
The patterns of a summer's day.
A masque 'low *Henry's little keep
Upon the waters lapping deep,
A dance as fresh this day in time
Just so it was in Tudor's clime

To sit and feast the ear and eye
Beneath an azure cloud brushed sky,
'Tis nourishment that sets the day,
Help act a part in this love play.
Press forth and on for more repast
Under the spell this beauty casts,
Sup deep the mead at nature's bench
Until my time on earth is spent.

*Henry VIII[th's] Castle, St. Mawes

Carne Sands

Upon Carne Sands I stood and faced
The thieving tide as in it raced,
The surfing wave with salt soaked mane
Raced landward to consume its gain.

It stripped the marram at cliff's base
Then stole the soil from its face,
Channelled rocks funnelled the streams
So froth beat sea there swirled and gleamed.

The river found its way reversed
In battle with the roaring surf,
There trees took were the soil met sand
Where blasted back upon the land.

Warring sea smote twig and branch
Used limbless trunks to form a rank
Foundation for its steepened beach
The rivers force can't even breach.

The little bridge that spanned the stream,
Where lotus eaters summer dream
And lie on sunlit yielding sand
Is crushed and stolen with its land.

The pathway 'long the *Pink Hotel
Beneath the raging waters fell,
Swept away after decades
A victim to the seas fresh rage.

So in one storm this little world
Transformed as waters fury hurled
And sculpted out in just one night
All access man made by his might.

*Hotel overlooking Carne Beach

The Hunter in the Woods

Well met sir, in this silent wood
Where I seek verse and you seek blood,
I knew you were not far from here
Your gun spoke loud, its message clear.

I judged your day was a success
I found a pheasant in distress,
The shot you fired had pierced its eye
Surprising that it did not die.

Hung there you have six that are dead
Their lovely plumage sodden red,
They fell like hail from up on high
The sky's highway on which they fly.

When you arrived here on the lane
I knew your interests dealt in pain,
You think your gun's a lovely thing,
Though nought but death for birds it brings.

Of course it's only birds you kill
Just little murders give you thrill,
Here for your quarry skulk and hide
In this lovely countryside.

These creatures that you hurt and maim
They're yours, you bred them for the game,
You put them in the wood and field
Power of death o'er them to wield.

You're not alone in this delight
Your dogs they wag and rush and bite,
One fetched a bird with gaping wound,
Your equal joy, though he's a hound.

So good day sir, your repast's done
Time once again to take your gun,
Enjoy the horror game you play
I'll resume mine another day.

The Pools Dragonfly

The sky low grey, its grudging light
Gives little to my fading sight,
Deep shadows black with mystery,
Though whispering ferns have words for me.

The pool reflects its dying growth,
While metalled turquoise fleeting ghost
Hunts and haunts diminished prey,
Signals the end of sunlight's day.

Never again warm world of light
Giving brilliance to her flight,
The nourishing space now starved and cold
But still she lives her life as bold.

I've sat, observed this time before,
Seen deaths hand take one from the fore,
Watched a faltering flight still brave
End, plunged into a watery grave.

But in those depths her sinister child
Waits it's time to taste the wild,
To don its splendour, please the eye
Who loves to sit beneath the sky.

The trees and ferns that drink the deep
Where fishes lie through Winters weep,
Rest now my loves, for Spring will keep,
You safe when you awake from sleep.

A Life

There is a seat where often I sit
It faces woods and fields and sea.
They help inspire the words I fit
My little tributes to beauty.

Strange it must seem most every day
In sun and rain I'm at this bench.
Idle and solitary, there I stay
Pipe, book and pen my recompense.

Two darling little hairy hounds
To imposed rest must now resort.
Coffee flask sits on the ground
Its contents help ideas brought

Music feeds me loveliness
I try to maintain train of thought,
Sometimes easy, sometimes less
With pen and paper words are caught.

Small life of little consequence?
But mine, directed as I wish.
Honesty with no pretence
And never tiring of that dish.

Tide Times

Scimitar of the surf shines bright,
Curving down along the beach,
Blade in motion lighting white
Cutting in towards lands reach.

Here lying on a marram bed,
Watch light dying from the west,
See white winging shadows tread
Roosting islands where they nest.

Silent, save the whispering sea,
Mates the water to the earth,
Softly sings its song to me
A melody that's all of worth.

The walled shadow of the cliffs
Stands proudly on horizons seat,
It blends in darkness with the sea
As drowning sun gives light deplete.

Fitful dream how I begot
The man I am or soon at hand
Fixed not at this brief time spot.
Life motioned grain of sand.

The Walled Garden

High walled sanctuary for the green
Against which wood framed greenhouse leans,
To drink the sky.
Time weathered brick softened in form
To nest the bee away from harm
So that the nectar he can farm
And nightly lie.

Terraces of patterned brick
Surround the loam decades enriched
By loving toil.
Summers warmth and gardeners tide
Sit food and beauty side by side,
Cabbages and marigold pride
Deaths insects foil.

Fertile 'neath the bee's soft hum
They step their growth to life's paced drum
Like you or I.
And here the hoe and rake and spade
Has fruitful loving labour made
At nature's bounteous alter laid,
A calling high.

Winter Orchard

The frost is heavy on the ground
Steps marking crisp with whispered sound
And sun-bright cast across the grass
Has not yet strength its warmth to cast.

The apple trees are deep in rest,
No sign of bud yet manifest,
Greenhouse jewelled through the dark,
Sanctuary 'gainst colds killing spark.

Here Geranium flowers bloom,
Bright lit life through winter's gloom
Hymning softly to the light,
Pulsed with life in crimson bright.

The plank edged plot waits for the seed
That births the plants on which we feed
Lies sad deplete from winters take
The spade and fork soon it awake,

Old Summer House made versatile
To keep dry winters high log pile
Which daily trips eke out deplete
Against the cold to respite seek.

The dark green sentinels to the east,
Boundary so the wind won't feast
Upon the fruit the trees provide
When summer storms seasons deride.

And Sloe along the southern side
Leaf mantle safe 'gainst season's tides,
Its fruit now feeding sweet the gin
To cheer the firelight's night-time sin.

Here also fire had cheered the dark,
The embers still with smoke and spark,
Through night the bonfires dimming eyes
Saw fox and fowl 'neath cold star skies.

And so this little sanctuary
Where loving labour spirit frees
Will sleep beneath a blanket cold
Awake in Spring renewed and bold.

Robin Red

The little warrior on my seat
Emboldened by winters deplete,
He looks at me with deep jet eye
Seated beneath the leaden sky.

Wars he's fought and battles won
To win his place nearest the sun,
This little conqueror breasted red,
Who now befriends me to be fed.

The beak is sheathed, rested his knives
That pierced and ripped at other lives.
Though man may sentimentalise
He owns his all by blinding eyes.

This little king whom none may own
Ripped out feather, flesh and bone,
For last year's Robin now is dead
Murdered by this bird of red.

Now's the emperor of the lawn
The nearby copse is his to own,
Don't let his little frame deceive
He is the tyrant of the leaves.

So at my side he cocks his head,
He has a message to be said
"Now pay me quickly what you owe
And after from my kingdom go"!

The Buzzard

In majesty death floats on air
Victim's transfixed with upward stare,
Fingered wings each barred their length
His mewing song no recompense.

His sabre claws are fisted loose
Ready to pierce which e'er he choose,
His wild stare gaze detects each blink
From creatures now courage extinct.

He circles over with intent
Along his little firmament
Denying anything below
From his green clad kingdom go.

Then closing on him black and white
War with him their want to fight,
The gull and crow put by their fear
The buzzard has no terror here.

They swoop and mock and take his eye
Away from earth and to the sky,
Strike his wings his course to vex
A victim now, power annexed.

He calls defiance, shows his claws,
His harassment goes without pause
Until he speeds upon his way
To deal in death another day.

The Crow

Jet black eye with look ungentle,
Perched atop the green boughed mantle
Watching, seeing, pouncing, taking,
Love for nothing, birthed for hating.

Takes from me and robs from you,
Scaled, black feathered washed with blue,
The doors ajar in his hard life
Are those that lead to cold and strife.

Each dawned day his end predicted
Less he is to war addicted,
Less he hears that pillage call
And takes and takes and takes it all.

Look to the Mountains

The gales that stride the mountains high
Nights screeching terrible to our ears,
And yet the lowly fell land sheep
Sleep sound beneath dense cloud soaked sky.

And on the rocky barren heights
Where we would starve of nourishment
The raven black and glossy thrives,
There through stark winter spends his nights.

Red stags hold kingdom on those fells,
His hinds he guards and nurtures close,
In winter valleys clothed in snow
He moss and grass and gorse foretells.

In tumbling ice froze mountain streams
Sit golden trout in granite pools,
In summer gorged, in winter starved
But year on year the life force gleams.

Look to these mountains as your guide,
Your mother is the earth you tread,
Be not the teacher but the taught,
List' nature's song the whole world wide.

Bowland's Trough

On Bowland's Trough where as a child
We drove to see and taste the wild,
Find skylarks nests with gaping babes
Midst heather brightly purple hazed.

Our little Morris aged black
In its stride took roads and tracks
And on rear red crazed leather seat
I'd sit and view natures surfeit.

By the limestone river bed
Were Dippers twixt the runnels fed
And where the Pheasants in the fields
Sparred with beak and claw for yield.

Behind hedgeways ending fast,
Rabbit multitudes ate the grass
And each fresh view gave us a thrill
Of creature science plots to kill.*

As day ends lights final cry
A thousand Starlings mount the sky
Dance worship as in air they run
With dip and whirl hymn dying sun

Gulls that late o'er land had fed,
To roost to seaward islands sped,
Marking the climax to the play
We homeward to more mundane days.

myxomatosis introduced 1953

Mountain Skies

Cast my dust to fly in winds and fall in sunlit
bowers,
Sit soft upon the rivers bank through the infinite
hours,
Be blown about the mountains high, down in valley
deep,
And on the purple heathered slopes, soft to lie in
sleep.

O'er the paths to open skies where first I met my
soul,
Young and strong was there I trod, found all to
make me whole.
Now to kiss the Rowan red and on the Sloe's bed
lie,
Be frozen under winter's snow, freed by
springtime's sky.

My music carried on the wind where the curlews
cry,
Singing from the rushing stream as white bibbed
dippers ply,
Sleep enfolded by the love always before my eyes,
At last in my eternal rest 'neath the mountain skies.

Ruffian Wind

A ruffian wind is here today,
Its presence obtrudes every way,
This choristers song atop the trees
Creates a mood unsettles me.

The sun is weak and fails to rule
In conflict with this speeding cool
Air running over field and flower
Which keeps us in old winter's power.

There are some places it can't get
And I seek out where summers set
Its stall of warmth and salving light,
Where there's no wind to fight its fight.

A seat behind a granite wall,
That offers rest in sunlight's call,
No motion there where calms the thing,
Listening to the wild air sing.

And added to this Spring time warm
A steaming cup and pipes my norm
And there's a role for me's been found
To keep amused my pestering hounds.

Now for an hour and constantly
I throw a stone for she and she,
Devious so to give some time
To sit and think and write my rhyme.

And thus the days they roll along
As I unite to my word song,
A simple song, a simple man
A dance to the best tune I can.

Never to let complacency
Or worse the curse of vanity
Deceive to think my rustic prance
In rhyme or verse has much advance

When loud I whistle in the wind
Its nought against the breezes sing,
My tune is lost in that broad air
Symphonic sound is everywhere.

But on my triangle I'll play,
A tiny sound in rhythmic sway,
My role is just a little note
That my composer for me wrote.

Winters Demise

The long sad sigh of winter's breath
That greys the fields, of life bereft,
Keeps blind with the diminished light
Where nature's eye has lost its bright

A cold keep blanket of the cloud
With ice cut air beneath the shroud,
These constant in oppressive clime
Where deep is sleep as death defined.

High up above this leaden sky
The infinity of the azure lies,
A bed, reposes there the sun
This world is his, the war long won.

High rising soon to rule again
Astride his mount with fiery main
Through swirling mists of melting cold
Give Sun's child summer lease to hold.

Claustro

Down in the valleys subdued light
My eyes look to the mountains heights
And though I'm in a sheltered place
I want the high winds on my face,
I want to tread those airy ways
Where ravens fly and Herdwick's graze
And they the only company
In that high world that's people free.

The sense of freedom in that space
Where high winds blow upon my face
Is anchored somewhere deep inside
Where many other senses hide.
The sound or unsound inner man
Constructed by my whole life's plan
That's made of circumstances chance
Or some divine deliverance.

And only on those mountains high
Beneath the blessed spacious sky
Can I breathe deep affirming air,
Knowing there's nothing fearful there?
No dark encasing earthy place
To smother air upon my face
And thus I love high places wild
That let this man escape the child.

Old Year

Cold March, though here is summers hand, warm
the touch upon the land,
Feeds optimism to reflect on what the year might
provide yet.
I'm almost there atop the hill sat in the sun with
time to kill
And though from its demands seem free, truth to
tell times killing me.

See clearly how it's quickened pace treads the lines
across my face,
Thins the hair and dulls the eye but I can still on
arts wings fly,
With love of rhyme and love of song, know with that
I can belong,
In my near horizoned life where close my heart
there points times knife.

Modus Vivendi

Up high the cold damp air is king,
With just the weak sun glistening
Upon the lately frosted grass
Through early morning fields I pass.

Down to the valleys darker land
Where trees and lakes in shadow stand,
Waiting for the nourishing light
To transform from the cold of night.

To stir the Rudd from out the deep
So at warm surface water seek
The nymphs and insects of the mud,
Awakened by the seasons bud.

And in their turn the fish is sought,
In silent motion herons stalk
With lightning strike and dagger beak
They snatch them from the sun blessed keep.

Close by, the moorhens muddy creep
Along the margins of the creek,
Shy and furtive so to hide
Where her nest and fledglings bide.

Bolder though in apron bright
Made brave by winters starving blight
A little warriors at a seat
To have his share if I would eat.

Now as the sun treads to the east
The woodlands sated with its feast,
Life awakes from its long lie
To keep its modus vivendi.

A Song Of the Dead

The books they read were of the past
Of heroes charging to the last,
Of native men in native lands
Defeated by the heroic band.

Of horses, sword and flashing lance
In tunics red danced victories dance,
So when for them the bugled called
They had no fear of battles pall.

The great adventure lay before
These lambs they flocked to go to war,
Their families proud to see their sons
In khaki ranks with sloping guns.

They knew they'd see them soon again
A short sojourn to make them men,
No man an island stood alone
Comradery that bore them on.

With merriment and many a joke
Ever closer to deaths cloak
And soon the rage of battles flow
Engulfed them in their minion role.

A tiny speck of living dread
Atop the pyramid of the dead
The ground around them seething black
With blood and bone and pain is racked.

The friends in arms who comfort brought
Gone as death for each man sought,
The great machine of war rolled o'er
With splintering steel and deafening roar.

Widows wept and parents grieved,
Lost their sons so sad deceived.
The fattened vultures in their nests
Perch, profits from the dead to rest.

And singing anthems on your feet
Be sure continues that deceit
The pinnacles of the opposing sides
Wore crowns that still today divide

Don't sing of justice, or of right,
Nothing nobles in the fight,
Brave heroes all who sacrificed
Gave all they had in precious life.

And if that multitude from death
Could sing a message of bereft
It sure would echo near and far
"Never again loves go to war"

Flying in Heaven

To love and not to sanctify
Like blackened clouds o'er sea and sky.
It foils the joy and dries the heart
To poison every tiny part
Of a sick writhing entity,
Another human lost at sea.

Love, to live and bear that name,
Across ethereal heights should plane,
Not footed in a sordid earth,
Blind and poisoned at its birth.
Mind and body have their role
To heighten joy to make us whole.

Each day as our sad earth slow turns
Its foibles in our minds are burned,
Man seems desired to bathe in strife
Not seek the finer sides of life.
Loves eternal, always there
But needs the taking, needs the care.

The pessimistic view of life
Created by the shriven device
Of worship for some "other" place,
Buries deep the beauteous face
Of that which stands before our eyes,
Heaven is here so fly its skies.

Sea Breezes

Sea breezes warm, breath of the sun
When naked o'er the sea I'd run,
My little boat my sanctuary
In which I was convention free.

No burden of the tutting tongue
For I was firm and slim and young
And with my love so fair and fine
We'd wed our joy upon the brine.

Feed from the larder of the sea,
Drink the wine the sky gave free,
Buck and prance across the waves
Happy, happy, distant days.

Long Lost Love

Long, long, so long ago in that far land in
which I'd grow,
Unlike the rooms I wander now in stranger's
houses dark.
Lost life's spark, blind of eye, seeking the
bright torch of the sky.

My mother's image, captured spark, dim
seen in shadow, lost in dark,
In that old day when war had turned the
whole world grey.
Curse the loss that masks the light to tell me
if my life was bright.

She wears the symbols of the rhyme, a
floral dress for special times,
A trilby hat all ribbon-ed round and at an
angle, tight curls crown its jaunty set.
A crooked smile that I keep yet and lips to
kiss, come death for this.

An Ending

The moons glow softly lit our room last night
As watched you sleeping distanced from my
plight,
Longed to bring you close and kiss your
face,
Though that awaking would my love
disgrace.

Words blades of hate would strike deep to
my heart
And it would bleed loves life into the dark,
Then hopes old vision blinded in its rove,
Descend into the grave of our dead love.

Distanced Hills

Stare from the steel framed window,
Out over the councils roofs,
Across dead mines and slag heaps,
Through factories poison ooze
And the river that they shat in,
Made a lifeless stinking corpse,
Near clearer confined water
Where barges profit wrought.
Over the terraced houses,
There the old and cold wheel prams
Of coke in exchange for spouses
And for sacrifice of lambs.
Where grey men crouched on doorsteps
Scoured white against gossips chat,
Course coughing out their life blood
Mixed to coal dust that they spat.
There far away in the distance
Are the Pennines' rolling hills,
Taunting a shout of freedom
To the poor chained to the mills.

Snowdrops

Across the orchard green from winters rain,
The treading sun leaves blessings in its train,
Awakening from sleep in earthy bed,
The modest little snowdrops shy white head.

So delicate a flower yet full of might,
Late winter's storms may yet smother the light,
But still this little angel of the Spring
Will dance the woods to make our spirits sing.

Who is it comes?

Who comes to me at dead of night?
On winds sigh in the cold moonlight,
Framed in the doorway naked stands,
There beckons me with death white hands.

I rise and lift her in my arms
To hold her close and make her warm,
Carry her to my soft bower,
To worship through the long night hours.

Lying entwined in close embrace,
The moonlight falls upon her face,
I look into her wide dark eyes
And see in there two serpents writhe.

Transfixed with terror by her side,
One arm around my body glides,
The other snakes across the floor
To turn the key that locks the door.

Summer Music

Loves music is the gentle breeze,
Singing its wind song through the trees,
There where the sun and leaves combine,
To robe the woods in light sublime.

It is the skies soft warmth and grace
Kisses the summer to my face,
Look distant sea between the slope
Of grass and hedgerows interlope

And in the valley, roading fast,
The crystal river runs its last,
Before it melts into the brine
To be a part of the divine.

The Sun

The warming sea has cloaked the land
In watery mist and stayed the hand
Of that great source of life and light
Beyond the grey still burning bright.
Waiting alone I face the shore
To feel loves warm embrace once more,
To glance it on its sapphire throne,
Its presence means no more alone
But now to share that gift to earth
Bestowed upon it since its birth,
Wrapped in its life enhancing grace
To feel the breath from heavens face

The Trout Stream

I love the beauty of this stream
Its crystal water curving gleams,
Clear and cold as rain washed air
It combs and twirls green tresses fair.

Where soft walled alleys gently wave
Are gravelled paths, the trout's highway,
Armoured gold up red eyes gaze
To sip the mayfly to its grave.

I wade and stalk in silent hunt
To cast my lure to his front,
To gentle mock his quarries flight,
Softy on the stream alight.

See revealed his rippled deceit
Where he is hid to find his meat,
Where sets his ambush in the weeds,
Hiding, watching, 'fore he feeds.

My tinselled disguise of a fly,
Delicate beckons to his eye,
He rising, swoops to have his way,
Now the hunter 'comes the prey.

Darting swift and strong in flight
His twisting body gives the fight,
In time his way he cannot get,
Across the current to the net.

His beauties stunning to the eye
I am not here to have him die,
I seek him here for life's bright gleam,
Go little fish back to your stream.

The Moon

It seems a deceit of the light,
In the day, the Queen of the night,
She sits as in a dream untrue,
Drowning slowly in the blue.

Gently moves toward the east
To sip where sun had gorged its feast.
Her deep black robe with shining gems
Divested out her own true realm,

Now lost within the azure skies
Her pale lit face as naked flies
Go rob the sun and give day flight
Open the doorway into night

Pike o' Stickle

The airs cut sharp and cold today,
The sky a mottled cloak of grey
Helmeting the tumbling screes
Of blasted rock from rain and freeze.

Some spoil here from ancient man,
Who in dank caves worked to his plan,
Did spear and arrow from rock hue,
Which at the mighty mammoth threw.

My path is high above the vale
Down where the snaking river rails,
Airy space below my feet,
Above me comes the rain and sleet.

The mist descends and wraps around
My world reduced to footfall sound,
Before, at rear, to left and right
The mist a sightless cloak of white.

But where my vision is made blind
The mountains song seems sound refined,
Hear myriad brooks that bleed the tops
And vein moss filtered crystal drops.

Splash and stutter over stones
Sculpted smooth with ages bones,
Converging, falling, rippling bright
Gifts the valley from the heights.

But then soul lifts beyond the skies
There comes a vision tears the eyes,
A pool of golden sun fed light
Reveals a beauty pure and bright.

Lights shafts tear away the veil,
Peeps the mountains plateaux pale,
No place on earth I'd rather be
As nature hymns eternity.

My Wife's Granny

All my life I've fondly thought
Of precious lessons that she taught
A little girl with sparkling eyes
Who loved her Granny old and wise.

At weekends when the world was free
She fed and loved and nurtured me,
I felt protected there and warm,
With my Granny safe from harm.

She built a path for me to walk
Throughout my life by lessons taught
And on that path when I look back
I see her waving by the track.

Her house a refuge from a Dad
Whose temperament was mean and bad,
My mother's life filled to the brim
With house and kids but mostly him.

I don't know why he meant us harm,
His presence filled us with alarm,
Four girls, two boys and ne'er a hug,
A cuff perhaps, this family thug.

But at my Granny's life was bright,
I sang and played into the night,
She cuddled me her darling child
And read me stories that beguiled.

I had an innocence she loved,
Her little angel from above,
She recognised how much I cared,
Intimate feelings always shared.

Her standards routed in a time
Before our country had declined.
Convictions based on wrong and right
The good fight fought with all her might.

Her world is gone and so is she
Into that great eternity
But in my heart she'll never die
She waits for me beyond the sky.

Standish

This neat but oil stained concrete ramp,
Here as a babe I sat in rank
With cousins, friends on either side,
Swimming 'gainst the encroaching tide.

The soot stained water's swirling black
Had drowned my mother some way back
And here 'fore concrete on dried mud
We played alone and drank worm's blood.

Such horrid children to the eye
But war kept food in short supply,
Hunger's dark and makes uncouth,
The mind 'comes secondary to the mouth.

Terraced houses either side
In which the "working classes" bide,
A belt and braces deprived world
Where light ale and tobacco swirled.

Where social standings always kept
Judged by the whiteness of her step
And marriage means two separate lives
Through spying windows, judging wives.

Men gather playing gambling games,
You pass them furtive in the lanes,
All watchful for law's petty vice
To spend their leisure throwing dice.

Cathedral ruins blind of eye,
Coals churches open to the sky,
Sit beside the slags high mounds,
Waste from death below the ground,

Watching, waiting safe away
The open secret games they play
And when the last worn suit went hence
We'd search their sanctuary for pence.

Their every hour set to the pace
Defined from birth to deaths embrace,
Art or genius shackled close
Feared conventions haunting ghost.

Time moved on to make a choice;
Discordant choir or solo voice,
Accept the norm or free the mind,
Open eyed or shackled blind.

Set to voyage and seek the grail,
Before refreshing breezes sail,
New horizons, don't look back,
Towards freedom make your tack.

A Lancashire Childhood. 1946

There are some things I'd rather hide,
Reality I just keep inside.
Don't want to go back to that place
Where last I saw my mother's face.

I was too young to "know" the war,
Coals allegiance to which men swore.
My only memory is of Yanks
On Castle Hill in rattling Tanks.

Too many there the world was bleak,
Short and steep on Bleakledge Street.
And one of them was my dead mum,
Lost giving birth to a stillborn son.

My father as a soldier fought,
His visits home were few and short
And just as he resumed his life
Death came along and stole his wife.

It left him with a stranger child,
Motherless and unreconciled,
Dad's sister in the house next door
Responsibility she now bore.

Viewed now through the haze of time
Emotion's mountains hard to climb,
Lonely, lost, no guiding hands,
A little stranger in his land.

Compensations made thing worse,
Pedal car, but of love a dearth,
Always feeling in the way,
Another bill Dad had to pay.

Hard men moulded by their world
Of Mill or Pit, tobacco swirled
In brown toothed mouths with eyes ringed black,
My uncle was a man like that.

I cannot think of just one time
When in his house his eyes caught mine,
Then yet again at five years old
Was ushered to another world.

Still a terraced back to back
With new strangers to set the track
On which my life and terrors ran
Foundations laid to make the man.

An error that we easily make
View the child's mind to awake,
As every parent sure has found
Instinct for love knows no bounds.

So the memory that haunts me still
From those dim dark streets by the Cotton Mill
Is the huge black void of loving's lack
So no, I really don't want to go back.

Childhood in the 50's

To many it seemed like a dark wasteland,
It spoke adventure to me and my friends,
Where Hop-along Cassidy rode his mare
And Tonto often encountered him there.

There Robin Hood oft' with his crew,
His mighty bow made from old bamboo,
Would rush across red fired slag heaps
And on the back of a horse would leap.

Then there'd follow a sort of a scrap,
The chosen horse began to fight back,
So then Flash Gordon would sort it out,
Giving the equine a bit of clout.

For some reason I'll never know
The horse seemed always to own the bow,
So he'd take it home in a fit of pique,
We'd abandon Sherwood for that week.

Nature sometimes took a clout,
Not all us kids were little boy scouts
And looking back I'm quite ashamed
At some of the Big White Hunters games.

On slag a red bricked castle stood
With a ladder made from pit head wood,
Once climbed it gave a harrowing peep,
Open mineshaft thousand feet deep.

Across its mouth was a mighty beam
And as unbelievable as it seems,
One of the braver, really not me,
Walked that beam above eternity.

They certainly were more innocent days
When weekends under the sun's bright rays
We'd let our imaginations loose,
Better than boring realities truths.

Looking Back

Rewind, rewind and let me be
That little child happy and free
Who skipped and held his mother's hand
In that far distant long lost land.
In woods and fields beside the farm
There was no fear of loss or harm,
We lay in corn under the sky
And watched where hymning skylarks fly.

Rewind, rewind so once again
A youth a maid's heart tries to reign.
In love, deep smitten, filled with joy,
I wish once more I was that boy.
I wish in alleys I could walk
And kiss and touch and laugh and talk
And in a bed lose innocence
And wake with scent of love intense.

Rewind, rewind and let me be
Again in that lost sanctuary,
A young man happy with full life
Of friends and work and future wife.
Warm sandstone, stained glass Gothic place
Of gentle folk at gentle pace,
Those times the gateway to my life,
To love, to joy, sadness and strife.

St Wilfred's Bells

On Sunday when I lay in bed
With last night's whiskies in my head
Across the avenues and streets
St Wilfred's bells pealed out their keep,
Their sound that sang a song for God
Rang all around the lives we trod.

Geese in passage roading by
To clear the Pennine moorlands high
Heard pulsing through the freezing air
The chiming, tolling signal there,
They answered with their mournful cry
Discourse with man from lonely sky.

Down in a dark nightmarish dream
The sound of bells masked o'er the screams
Of murder done by bloody knife,
A jealous husband to his wife,
Their child an orphan in the street
The peals unceasing rhythmic beat.

Down the lane below the hill
Young lovers strolled and for each thrilled,
The bells filled space where love would talk
So with embrace they ceased their walk
And lay amongst the ripening wheat,
To dance loves dance to bells repeat.

Three sisters heard the bells instruct,
Don finest clothes and come to cluck
And crow the hymns the curate set
And from him some attention get.
Each trampled on their siblings need
To marry to the clergy's creed.

And me, I stumbled down the stairs
To live a life where no-one cares,
To route amongst the unwashed cups
Imbibe life's blood, towards death sup,
Closed tight the windows in my house
So church bells didn't have a voice.

Miners. 1926

A side street short atop the hill
Where dark in soot's festooning kill,
Fractured brick of blackened red
Housed the coal-mines living dead.

The night had hours yet to lie,
Sleepwalking men with black rimmed eyes
Stooped in motion in the streets
Where iron soles tapped out defeat.

Each man hiding he was owned
For all his life to be a drone,
To work or starve the simple choice
A chorister without a voice.

The choirmasters far away
We're looking how to cut their pay,
To make them toil a longer day,
Men recent war put in harm's way.

Men who'd answered brave the call,
Hailed heroes by nation enthralled,
Comrades killed in stench and stink,
Deserted now and at the brink.

The politicians there to serve
Give justice to these men of nerve,
Patted them as they were dogs
Then at the trough fed with the hogs.

So when you read the Daily Mail
And with it against poor men rail
You stand in rank with those vile pigs
Who for the noble graves did dig.

Sleep

Sleep come to end the weary day,
Dark melt the pain and hurt away,
Let this mattress where I lie,
Assume the softness of the sky,
Make sensation on my face
Be numb to pillows sleep deface,
I at life's table want no seat
In this world where love's deplete.

Guardians

"That's my bus that's pulling out
I must be home or Dad will clout",
Dashed from the path into the road
Then felt an arm around me fold,
The lorry's brakes loud in my ear
As I was pulled and lifted clear,
Rescuer stared into my face,
Nothing sensed but my disgrace,
Others there with comments loud,
Mute he turns, melts in the crowd.

Shear and high the granite rock
As I ascended for the top,
The nuts and wedges there to save
Lifted, ran down to my grave.
The routes increasingly extreme,
At the crux the end it seems,
Muscles tired and start to shake
On tiny holds I sweat and quake.
But then my saviour, a top rope!
A brother climbers dropped me hope.

New confidence, the crux I climb
Then up the final pitch I grind,
I look ahead for a view of he
Who's given me alacrity,
Action that had saved my life,
Loved, not a widow still a wife.

And now the climbing's really grand
I cannot wait to shake his hand,
I climb up to encircling air,
Rope is fixed, there's no-one there.

The sea is running fast and high,
A full eight knots we homeward fly,
Despite it being wind 'gainst tide
We buck and skip, but safely ride.
Surreal like, the motion stops,
"God! We've fouled roped crab pots"!
We hang there like a gull on air
I rush below, a knife is there,
Hack and curse against this strife
But suddenly we have new life!

The taut rope that's of such concern
Lifts the rudder off the stern,
The boat restrained now flies freed
But there's no way to steer or lead.
The cliffs at distant from our bow
Are getting ever closer now,
But then we see with huge relief
Our rescuers, the "FT Pentreath".
She tows us to the estuaries calm,
Fixed to a buoy won't come to harm.

The strangers are men of the sea
Deep tanned as fishermen will be,
They've more to offer in our plight
See if our rudder they can sight.
Within the hour they are returned
Our rudder fixed on pintles firm,
No recompense or salvage fee,
Wave farewell and out to sea.
Falmouth conversing at the bar,
"Pentreath was lost boy in the war"!

Love's sad song

I haunt within your fragrant trail,
I love but trail to no avail,
I cry avail deep in the night,
I burden night with your delights.

You do not know how deep I care,
You do not care when I'm not there,
You are there for other love,
You love another, oh sweet dove,

We together never apart,
We never are apart in heart,
We could our hearts through time embrace,
We never will embrace loves grace.

My Mistress

I walk upon a path of gold
With diamonds spark alive in air,
Soft breezes warm me naked there
And all around me heavens doors.
Caressing hands, enfolding arms
As on a bed of softest balm,
Enveloped by a lovely form
Caressing as no woman can,
For music is my mistress here
God's art created here by man.

A Mothers dream of Beloved Ones

Last night I had a vivid dream
I saw my Granny so it seemed
And in her arms so softly borne
My little children safe and warm

My female child dark and petite,
 Her smiling countenance so sweet
My darling tiny fair haired boy
Embraced his sister with sweet joy

As granny kissed each little face
She said "We'll wait here in this place,
Play my loves be bright and gay,
One day your mummy comes this way".

I woke from sleep with new found hope
To face my life with broader scope
To live and love and journey on
Knowing someday we'd all be one.

My Dog Coco

"Its fifteen years that we've been pals,
We've walked some miles on our travels,
My little legs have coped so well
On Cornish path or mountain fell.

We've been out there most every day,
With stick and ball I've loved to play
And even though I'm called a Dach
I've never liked it on a lap.

You've got a theory, this I know,
That exercise has helped me grow
Fit and happy, the years enhanced
By our constant happy dance.

But now old man we're slowing down,
Both going blind, limping around
Familiar paths at Heligan,
Now one of us must take the van.

No not a vehicle silly man
But take the initiative if you can,
Otherwise a walk I'll barr
And stay behind sat in the car.

I can't do that in the old MG
There's not enough security,
So then you wont be able to swank
You like to pose you daft old crank

You knew this day would have to be
You bought a sling to carry me,
There's rumour that you bought a pram
You're going to look a silly man.

You'll walk around, Granddad self-styled,
Folk will look to see the child,
Instead of baby smiley and pink
A hairy face and a bit of a stink.

I think for now the pram we'll leave
Just carry me in that nice soft sleeve,
The exercise will do you good
In no time you'll be less of a pud.

So carry the sling, carry the bag.
Millie on a lead, it might seem a fag,
I love you dad, it's worth the try
You'd like to be the first die!"

My Dog Millie

"Throw me a stone dad I'm getting bored,
No use pretending, won't be ignored,
Sitting sucking on your smelly pipe,
Do something useful don't sit and write.

I'm on a lead fastened to this bench.
I've been very patient but that's well spent,
Coco's bored now she's licking my face,
Tongue's in my ear, it's a real disgrace.

Doing that to mum she might appreciate
Titillation from an old ingrate.
laughing cynically when you offer her a bone!?
That won't happen on this bench,
So Dad please throw a stone!"

Hindley, Lancs in the '40s

1942 alive, by 1946 deprived
Of mother, brother, home and life
Out in a world depraved through strife,
Dark the streets and dark the folk
Like ghosts in coal mines bondage yolk
They stumbled in a blackened world
Of soot wet streets were death smoke swirled

No pity their or loving care,
Slaveries hand gripped everywhere
To strangle hope and gasp despair.
Men died slowly on their steps
Diseases fingers through them crept,
The pavement scattered with their blood
Spat from their lungs mixed in black mud.

And industry defined the clime
On death quiet days when yellow slime
Exchanged for air o'er all did wind
Your whole world close and wrapped around,
Unseen the set twixt sky and ground,
Sounds magnified in density,
Sense poised for some eternity.

Children tried to find some joy
Before their time for ages cloy
Deprived them of some greater goal
Enslaved for life to black gold coal.
Looking back oft some will say
"Do you recall the good old days"?
I then know we walked different ways.

Child in Darkness

I shade my gaze from present way to view a distant
earlier day
When as a child I occupied space in a world
entirely died.
I try to see who's in a room, dark shadowed by
distances gloom,
From where my elder cousin led us candle lit up to
our bed.

And from the top on that dark stair look down to see
if mother's there,
Oh why, oh why can I not see the face of who gave
birth to me?
Easier be to live the lie that I shall meet her when I
die,
Why trust that fate to reunite what once it took
when life was right.

What was I then I do not know, how did I cry or
miss her so,
Lies can be stories kindness writes but what I
seek's revealing sight.
The words lie here upon the page, I would not feel
this inward rage
Had I been given words to light the darkness of my
childhood's night.

Along the Ringing Alleys

Along the ringing alleys where he courted in sweet
thrall,
laid open his heart's wishes to the one who was his
all
and she listened, she glistened like a silent jewel
there,
the light that she transmitted blinded him to lack of
care.

She lived along those alleys where clog irons rang
a song
late night and early morning as the pitmen walked
along
to the coalmines at the lights birth, from pubs as
daytime died
at the rear of terraced houses that alleyways allied.

Fair Jean, a face of beauty, proffered gifts of love
and care,
he took the care and loved it as it came from one
so fair,
but in the alley gateways insincere she took his
heart
possessed it for a keepsake, left despairing in the
dark,

A red bricked terraced cottage deeply shadowed in
the night,
with dim lit little outhouse shone by gas flames
flickering light,
from there a crimson ribbon flowing down along
the yard,
into the ringing alley love congealing cold and hard.

Hollow Man

There stands a hollow man,
Flaunts an empty heart,
Words substitute for thought.
Pity a world in his care,
There is only vanity there.

There stands a hollow man,
Seeks battle where there's peace,
Disguised pride and contempt,
Deceiving pointless cant,
Domination is his rant.

There stands a hollow man,
Wrings hands in deceit,
Quicksand 'round his feet,
Blindfolded eyes can't see,
God keep from you and me.

Good and Evil

There's more than just one side to me,
The man you get's not what you see,
We all project our deep desires
To those to love we do aspire.

The singularity oft defined
Simplification from the mind
Of complex, varied human kind
That only the creator could define.

Evil and goodness hand in hand
Stalk all the world, martyrs to hand
For both can birth the others child
Division is not sanctified.

Who We Are

My mind and its complexity,
That is what is meant by "me".
The body lying on the bed,
Inconsequential, feet of lead,

Strength and pleasure to provide,
Diminished now by time resides.
But all of this can overcome
If me is unbound, free to run,

So take the logic I project
And even if you're circumspect
If that free mind is truly "me"
Its words are its identity

Comes the Dark

I need not look to see the sky
Encircling me around and high,
On wind song days the woods and trees
Play soft their sweet old melody,
I hear, I feel, I need not see

The poppies red no eyes to sense
If sun or moon gives recompense,
Yet if the earth in quiet does lie
Know queen of night is in the sky.
I hear, I feel, I need not spy

My life long through my eyes were blessed
To give my soul poetic rest,
The suns death kiss, his burning lights
Embraced away my failing site.
I hear, I feel, I'll can't fate fight

A book of chapters is our life,
Tales of love live side of strife
But until deaths knell loud I hark
I won't relinquish life's bright spark.
I'll hear, I'll feel until the dark.

Faith Distorted

What the faith that fosters hate
Enough to kill and mutilate.
What the faith destroys the good
Soaks the earth in innocent blood.
What the faith intolerance makes
A love for war for war's own sake.
That same faith that seeks divide,
Man from man on opposite sides.
What the faith that blinds the eyes
To the humanity it denies.
What faith is it debases each?
Committed to extend its reach
It is not faith that sets this course
But planned distortion of its source.
Faith should exist to raise up man,
Support his living where it can,
Progressive, not to set us back
A thousand years along the track.

Man Begone

Man begone, no more disgrace
This world, this nature you deface,
Your greed and merciless exploit
Has driven all the beauty out.

Unwelcome thief, naught was your gift,
Debased mind, you made the rift
To rape and kill the forest wild,
A playground for your sinful child.

Your generations are a curse,
Tenants, with diminishing worth,
Destroyers of the creator friend,
Love spurned, warrants now an end.

Beyond horizon out of sight,
There comes a darkness of the light,
You never lit from natures spark
Go to your home, eternal dark.

Guardian Angel

I trod the path between the trees
That ranked and shed their dying leaves,
I thought I heard a light footfall
Behind me in the dusk lights pall.

Dared not look but faced ahead,
Body and mind consumed with dread
Then softly whispering in my ear
Their spoke a cracked voice soft and clear,

"The clock you hear with quickening chime
My footsteps pace to mark its time
But when I link your arm with mine
One touch and you are lost to time"

"To walk a path towards your God
And cast away this earthy sod,
I'm your dark angel here to bless
To bear you onwards to your rest".

"I've been here through the rolling years
My governance of joy and tears,
You've felt me near each time you've said
There is no life when I am dead".

"I am the mystery in your life
That guarded you through times of strife,
Enclosed you in my warm embrace
When tears and sadness marked your face".

"Your sins are yours I had no part,
Each sin tore deep into my heart.
Not I to judge the life you led
I tried my best to guide your head".

"My voice was conscience through your time
Oft loud or silenced for each climb,
But for each milestone in your life
Together on that road we strived."

"You've viewed through misted lens unclear,
But soon the time is drawing near
When you will die beneath the sky,
Mystery solved to that great... WHY "?

Long Winter's Eye

Too long I've stared in Winter's eye
Of cold and rain and low grey sky,
This little refuge on the hill
Surrounded by all natures thrill.

Too long to listen to its cry
From howling winds around my lie,
Awakened through the restless night
Forced witness to its noisy flight.

Too long to long for seasons end
And visions walk with my sun friend
Across the clear hope sky of dawn,
With fields long shadowed, bright lit drawn.

To step into a bathing warm
That cleanses all of winters harm,
Floats off the mantle from my strife
Restores belief in kinder life.

Humanity

How do you think your paths defined
As on the road through life you grind,
Is it chance dictates your way
Or some divine leads every day.

Is this world designed for you,
Your God providing for the few,
A single species on the earth,
Nine million others lesser worth.

Is this why you trample down
Because you wear the kingdoms crown,
Not just the image of a God
But rule this place with iron rod.

You are a scourge upon this earth
Destruction ever since your birth,
You kill and ruin every day
In sick and selfish games you play.

Your gains are all around yourself
To keep you here in greater health,
Prolong the agony of this orb
As more of you it must absorb.

You cannot share you must have all,
Your wisdom might yourself enthral,
But your creations all your days
Can't match the sunset's fiery blaze.

Genius

Hear Burton, Thomas to recite
Magnificent "Dying of the Light",
I know my verse is earthy sod
Beneath the feet of giants trod.

But each of us can but aspire
And not let genius make expire
Our little tributes through the art,
However far we are apart.

Music

Nothing lifts my spirits so high
As music's sweet soliloquy.
Care not for genre it's the same
If melodies in beauties name.

I think my thoughts and write my words
To filter them through music heard,
Immersed in finer things of life,
In solitude there is no strife.

The woods and paths waltz to a tune,
The scene around more brightly blooms,
For this for me of all of the arts
Goes more directly to my heart.

Permeates all and paints the day
With colour bright to cover grey
And drunk with it as light departs
I'll dance and sing into the dark.

The Spectre

That spectre glanced beyond the door,
What were those strange dark clothes he wore?
They streamed with crimson green and gold
Where barbed adornments held the folds.
The cloth was soaked in human tears,
The spectres skeletal body clear,
Defined by how the garment clung
Across his bony shoulders flung.
He had attached around his waist
A rusting sword by blood defaced.
The sockets where would be his eyes
In there, two painted serpents writhed.
His toothless jaw dropped to entreat
The scream pitched voice called "trick or treat"!!?

Take Out Your Book

"Take out your set ideas book"
I'll bet its minutes since you looked,
It's such a really useful tome
There should be one in every home.

What is wrote in indelible ink,
Saves you ever having to think.
It covers all you need to know
And the confidence to say it's so.

Let's find a topic for today
And see what we can safely say,
There's standard things to say on race
Based on the colour of a face.

And children there you'll see defined
So our control can be refined.
On old people theirs lots of print,
Senility, sphincters, "don't they stink"?

Women at home, men at work,
There's nothing that this volume shirks,
Many revisions of the book
Updated for a modern look.

Young people have the latest edition,
Getting familiar with its tradition,
Theirs some new prejudice and clack
But mainly stays on the same old track,

But given time all they will learn,
Regurgitate it turn on turn,
To others the wisdom of the age
Because they are on the same page.

Hope Springs

The dense dark mantle of the clouds
Is lifted now from muted night
For weeks lain o'er us like a shroud
Blue sky now reflects colours bright.

Spirit stifled by the cloud
Now life is given back its spark
Can sing its joy with anthem loud
Emerging from cold winters dark.

Growth once dormant, hid away
Signals to the encroaching night
Peeps from buds in earth's round play,
Season's darkness will take flight.

So soon will come benignant days
We'll live and love and be as one
When once again in suns bright blaze
Taste nature's bounty ''neath the sun.

The Poet's Son.

I owe my father quite a lot,
That drunken idle genius sot,
He taught me work regard a sin
If I was to take after him.

To happy be one had to laze
In dreaming alcoholic haze,
Avoiding energetic fright
Except embracing in the night.

Of course because he didn't care
Women sought him everywhere,
My mother wild and free as he
She shared him most reluctantly.

She first all met him at the pub
Which he thought as his private club,
The landlord's holidays each year
Dependent on dad's love for beer.

Despite his penchant for the can
Was above all a ladies man,
The girls surrounded him to drool
As he seduced from bar-room stool.

Accessed their knickers with his art,
Poetry and wit set him apart,
He was not by convention knit
His soul and spirit by it flit.

He took the words in most mundane
And fired them with eternal flame,
Transformed to art that Gods could claim
And gave the world a richer gain.

This Celt of jewelled beauteous fame,
Know I am of the meteors flame,
So when in dreams I seek my fee
His poetry is my legacy.

Life's Seasons

If each life season is to be
Joyful and fresh as hope to see,
Important not to carry on
Burdens from the previous one.

The drive for birth that marks the Spring
On Winter's nights is not the thing,
We all can love the fruits and flowers,
Less easy when frost rots the bower.

Smooth ripeness of the apples skin
Sits sadly after cankers sin
And what with relish once we'd eat
Will now make appetite deplete.

Life's sequence is for all to be,
It has through to eternity,
Make well of all that life designed,
Blinkered forward not behind.

Childish

On Castle Hill, atop the rise,
Beneath those coal smoke blackened skies,
Two little children watched up high
The starlings dance 'fore night-times lie.

The little girl with rag stripped hair
Sat close the boy with tousles fair,
Both captivated by the sight,
Forgot the fears of coming night.

A call to bed and holding hands
The little pair to nightmare land,
As candle lit they climbed the stairs,
To sleep a night of fear and cares.

Aside their room their brother slept,
From where to entertain he crept,
And acted out his nightly ploy,
Frightening the little girl and boy.

So childlike and so trivial seems,
This imposition on their dreams,
But such fed nightly in those years,
Foundation of a lifetimes fears.

The child should like a garden grow,
Nurture and love must always show,
For if we slight neglect the seed,
The lovely flower may grow as weed.

Afterlife

Are we like pebbles on the bed
Of a great lake when we are dead?
Did fate that chose to give us breath
Skim us forwards towards death
And our brief time of skip and flight
In sunshine's brightly warming light?
Propelled onwards, fading rings
Mark the surface as each wings
Towards a common destined role?
Do nephesh, jiva, atma, soul
Sink into dark eternal deep,
Cold stone, throughout all time to sleep?

A Choice

The rhythmic sound that sets the pace
Dictates the step of human race,
To some is like a beating drum
To others like a stuttering gun.

Some wish their life to wealth to mate,
The beat of time - accumulate!
Looking always in the purse
Material gains equal worth

Others, duty to a cause,
Treading onwards, never pause,
Grasp the duty, grasp the day,
Sweep dissenters from their way.

The killers of this world, war seek,
Disguise their sickness in its deep
Dark suffocating sins embrace,
Truth there is loath to show its face.

Others help their fellow man,
And be as positive as they can.
Dance in rhythm with the beat,
Healing acts and words to seek.

None of us fix to the divide
We all have faces that we hide,
All are all at times in part,
Best strive to have an honest heart.

If there's any truth writ here
Decide what in the world is dear,
Beneath which banner strive to march,
And in life's motion play a part.

Fear and Courage

Fear

Shallow breathe, shallow breath,
Shallow heart with shallow zest,
Silent go with silent tread,
Lest they hear thou art not dead.
Whisper quiet, whisper low,
Make no sound as through life go,
Fear the pack that circles thee,
Do not set their blood-lust free.

Courage

Breathe thou deep of life's great art,
Suck the milk sets thee apart,
Cry your name and shout your creed,
From your breast your life blood feed.
Fear not the suns bright light,
Call it down to warm your fight,
Face in battle, take attack,
Let not fears false conscience rack.

Life

Go live with man in harmony
The spirit unafraid and free.
Not to seek to go to war,
Not accept oppressions law.
Stand your place if stands alone,
Deaf to false conventions drone,
Look to see and watch the light,
Cast away from constant night.

Sam the Marathon Man

I had a friend who was to me the very best a friend
can be,
Loyal, warm and humorous, a Cornish Celt to truly
trust.
I see him now with smiling face, strong and fit to
win the race,
The problems of our working days diminished by
his winning ways.

An educator kind and caring, valued knowledge
always sharing
With his students, most who knew here was a
teacher strong and true.
His talent was to harmonize, fun and knowledge in
their eyes,
Humanity and Science combined, in this teacher
firm but kind.

And to his colleagues straight and true,
courageously expressed his view.
Pride of birth-right without rant or degrading bigoted
cant
Accepting without prejudice what lesser men turn
into vice.
So many people loved this man enchanted by the
web he span

And partnered by his loving wife he welcomed all

into his life.
Their table had the best of fare for this man had a
talent rare,

His cooking skills so finely honed that many a chef
would be dethroned
And proud I was he'd given me his life enhancing
gift so free

Through working days the course we ran deriving
strength to carry on,
His wise words influenced me to see the best time
when we both broke free
From routine life however worthy never a match for
freedoms journey
To find myself a new career that took me from this
friend so dear.

So circumstances and neglect reduced our contact
and respect
And though we met from time to time our friendship
suffered a decline
I never heard the steps of time approaching swiftly
from behind
To overtake him in his race and sickness claim this
man of grace.

I'm one of many this I know and not alone to miss
him so,
But I've no faith to ease the pain with promises of

heavens gain
The past is all that's of him left and I am of my
friend bereft
Life is a sadder, bleaker place never again to see
his face.

The Fire in the Room

The coal fires flame dances its joy,
Casts its merry shadows out,
The silent room with silent form,
Prostate waits quietus upon the couch.

A blanket portrays wasted limbs,
Atop it are the skin boned claws
That once caressed in love and care
Both child and lover, rain and night.

Those bright sparked eyes that laughed and cried,
Creative loves enticing door,
Stretched wider still views only walls
On which projected sees her all.

Amidst the scarlet pains retreat
She walks once more in woodlands green,
Nurses her child, kisses her loves,
Longs for a time that might have been.

And he who cares to whom she's all
Comes to her room away from cry
His silent scream as teacup falls
Dousing the firelights final sigh.

Look to....

Stare from the steel framed window,
over the councils roofs,
across dead mines and slag heaps,
'cross factories poisoning ooze
and the river that it shat in,
a lifeless stinking corpse,
below clear confined water
where barges profit wrought.
Over the terraced houses,
*where the old and cold wheel prams
of coke in exchange for spouses
and for sacrifice of lambs.
Where grey men crouched on doorsteps,
that are white 'gainst gossips chat,
course coughing out their life blood
with the coal dust that they spat.
There far away in the distance
are the Pennines' rolling hills,
taunting a shout of freedom
to the poor chained to the mills.

* Widows were given a winter coal or coke
allowance in the 40s

The Child in the Corner

A child in the corner, starving, wide eyed,
She clings to her baby who's already died.
Eating my dinner or drinking my drink
I just turn my back, I don't see, don't think
Get by with clear conscience, just close my eyes
Focus on things material that helps to disguise
A connection between us, not far the divide
From that room, that corner, that starving child

Who is that there?

Who is that person resting there?
Seated in my favourite chair,
He looks familiar in a way
Though older far and worn and grey.

He can't be him that lives in me,
He's much younger physically,
I see that old man's stamped by time
Whilst he in me's of modern clime.

That old man's carriage's stooped and small
Whilst he in me stands straight and tall,
Look how his face is furrow rent
His hands blue veined with fingers bent.

The man in me just yesterday
With wife and children bright and gay
Whilst that man there, sat in my home,
Long isolated and alone.

Those letters scattered on the floor,
Notes from the dead gone to the fore,
I recognise one from my friend
I see my mother's flowing hand.

Look at that album on his knee,
That man's steeped in adversity
Why does he weep a gentle cry?
 O'er images of days gone by.

My inner self loves all the world,
That man there looks stern and churled
But why is he sat in my clothes,
Why seated in familiar pose.
Time races fast away I know,
Though step a pace to with it go,
I'll keep my distance if I can
I never want to meet that man.

Billie Blue Boy

Auntie Eady's coming for tea you kids must
very careful be,
Your little cousin William must not be
pushed or run around,
Just leave him sitting quietly, [so he can die
before he's three]

And Billie enters with his mum all breathless
purple lipped and glum
And we all stare at this odd child with all the
humanity of the wild,
And wide eyed panting for his breath he
rests back on the knee of death.

And odd no cake and just a drink how
spoiled is this kid we think,
And no-one speaks, he stares ahead,
towards an assembly of the dead
And we all jolly out to play on Billie Blue
Boys final day.

Just Yesterday

Just yesterday the patriarch
Sat on the beach to watch the larks,
Parents and grandkids digging sand
A warm sun, stranger in the land.

No breeze to sap the gentle heat,
The sea far off with the tides neap
As I suck on a fat cigar
And witness Summer's door ajar.

Aback the beach a little hut
Specific for refreshment put,
Slowly filling as mid morn
The need for tea and scones is born.

The sea is creeping slow away,
Some rush towards in there to play
Then faster rush back to dry sand,
Reject cold waters freezing hand

And now the rock pools have their day,
Soliloquy has had its play,
With bucket, net and child to hand
Adventures in crab-nippy land.

The plastic buckets slowly stocked
With outraged tenants of the rock
Pools weed filled, sea deserted homes,
Each forced to have a little roam.

An hour of sequenced little shocks
Balanced on weed slippery rocks
And now it's time to reinstate
In pastures new the crab ingrates.

We glide back now on firm packed sand
To reclaim our oasis land,
Now circled closer than before
By lovers, haters, dogs and more.

The pull of home now beckons me,
I bid adieu and saunter free
From the foundations once I laid
When I was young and life was brave.

A Path to Cornwall

ABOUT THE AUTHOR

Frederick Howarth was born in Lancashire in 1942, a War Baby. By the time of his birth his father was serving with the Eighth Army in North Africa. Shortly after the end of the War, on his father's return to civilian life, "Freddy's" mother died in childbirth and he was left in the care of Aunts until he was eight when his father remarried and he returned to live with him.

Left school at 15 to work in numerous and diverse jobs but crucially at the age of 22 his work took him away from the North West to Bristol which became a springboard for his future life and where he met his first wife.

Encouraged by his then father-in-law, the Rev A.R.W. Gray of Tresillian, he pursued full time higher education which culminated in a University Honours Degree followed by teaching posts, first in Cumbria and later in Cornwall, where he has remained.

Divorced and remarried, he has two adult sons from his first marriage and three grandsons. A late convert to writing poetry which he embraced well after his retirement from teaching